First World War
and Army of Occupation
War Diary
France, Belgium and Germany

39 DIVISION
Divisional Troops
Divisional Cyclist Company
3 March 1916 - 30 April 1916

WO95/2574/2

The Naval & Military Press Ltd
www.nmarchive.com
Published in association with The National Archives

Published by

The Naval & Military Press Ltd

Unit 10 Ridgewood Industrial Park,

Uckfield, East Sussex,

TN22 5QE England

Tel: +44 (0) 1825 749494

www.naval-military-press.com

www.nmarchive.com

This diary has been reprinted in facsimile from the original. Any imperfections are inevitably reproduced and the quality may fall short of modern type and cartographic standards.

© Crown Copyright
Images reproduced by permission of The National Archives, London, England, 2015.

Contents

Document type	Place/Title	Date From	Date To
Heading	WO95/2574 Mar 16-Apr 16 39th Div		
Miscellaneous			
War Diary	Witley Camp	03/03/1916	03/03/1916
War Diary	Southampton	03/03/1916	03/03/1916
War Diary	Le Havre	04/03/1916	04/03/1916
War Diary	Le Havre Station	05/03/1916	05/03/1916
War Diary	Steenbecque	06/03/1916	06/03/1916
War Diary	Doulieu	13/03/1916	13/03/1916
War Diary	Wallon Cappel	24/03/1916	24/03/1916
War Diary	Doulieu	25/03/1916	25/03/1916
War Diary	Les Amusoires	16/04/1916	16/04/1916
War Diary	Essars	17/04/1916	30/04/1916
Miscellaneous	Appendix No. 7 Casualties		
War Diary	Casualties For June 1918		
Heading	186 Brigade RFA War Diary July 1918		

WAR DIARY or INTELLIGENCE SUMMARY.

(Erase heading not required.)

Army Form C. 2118.

39th Divisional Cyclist Coy.   VOL 1

VOL. 1 From March 3rd to 31st 1916

Place	Date	Hour	Summary of Events and Information	Remarks and references to Appendices
Witley Camp	3/3/16	8 A.M.	Left with instructions to proceed overseas	
Southampton	3/3/16	7 P.M.	Embarked on the S.S. La Marguerite.	
Le Havre	4/3/16	3:30 A.M.	Moved alongside the Quay.	
Le Havre	4/3/16	7:15 A.M.	Disembarked	
Le Havre	4/3/16	5:30 P.M.	Reached Rest Camp	
Le Havre Station	5/3/16	10:30 A.M.	Entrained for Divisional Concentration Area	
Steenbecque REF. Hazebrouck 1/100,000	6/3/16	7 A.M.	Detrained and marched Billets allotted at X roads N.E. of BOIS des huit RUES in the commune of WALLON CAPPEL	
DOULIEU	13/3/16	9 A.M.	Capt. R. McDougall, 2/Lt. R.J. Smith, and 2/Lt. V.C. Harris, 2/Lt. U.M. Bonnet and 30 N.C.O's and men left for a course of Instruction with the 8th Division	
WALLON CAPPEL	24/3/16	2 P.M.	Received orders to move to LES AMUSOIRES in the commune of ROBECQ	
DOULIEU	25/3/16	10 A.M.	The above mentioned officers & men returned to LES AMUSOIRES	
			The programme of work carried out by the Company during the period of March 6th to 31st consisted chiefly of general reconnaissance of all roads in the BETHUNE AREA also schemes in cooperation with Cavalry	

R. McDougall
Captain
Commanding 39th Divisional Cyclist Coy.

39 Cyclists
Vol 2

Army Form C. 2118.

WAR DIARY
or
INTELLIGENCE SUMMARY.
(Erase heading not required)

FROM APRIL 1st TO APRIL 30th 1916.

Place	Date	Hour	Summary of Events and Information	Remarks and references to Appendices
LES AMUSOIRES	April 1st / April 16		Reconnaissance and schemes in Co-operation with Cavalry.	
LES AMUSOIRES	April 17	8.30 a.m.	Company moved forward to ESSARS.	
ESSARS	April 17	11 a.m.	Arrived in new area at fork road E. of E in ESSARS	
Do	April 17/30		From April 17th The Company performed the following duties:- 17 men & 1 N.C.O were attached to the Divisional Signal Coy. 2 N.C.Os and 20 men to the A.P.M. for instruction in Traffic Control. 2 N.C.Os and 15 men on guards at certain points, beyond which no traffic is allowed to pass. The Divisional Bomb Stores is run by this company 1 Officer 1 N.C.O. and 1 man being employed there. The personnel of the Bombing School is also composed of Cyclists. (REF. BETHUNE enclosed sheet No.000)	

R. M. Dougall
Captain
Commanding 39. Divisional Cyclist Coy.

Appendix No 17 - Casualties

Date	Number	Rank	Name	Status	Unit
7-5-18	31935	Gnr	Payne T.	Wounded	A/186
9-5-18	66562	Sgt	Hey W.H.	— " —	B/186
17-5-18	45374	Gnr	Smith T.M.	— " —	D/186
14-5-18		A/Capt	A Hale	— " —	— " —
21-5-18	133609	Dr	Rankin J.	— " —	B/186
	48924	Gnr	Knight W.J.	Wounded At Duty	— " —
22-5-18	112172	Dr	Touracre J	Wounded	C/186
25-5-18	69098	Cpl	Simpson W	Injured	A/186
	831449	Gnr	Moody W.C.	Wounded	— " —
	109838	Bdr	Spacey S.	Wounded at duty	— " —
	86145	Gnr	Mumford F.C.	— " —	— " —
31-5-18	233685	A/Cpl	Saggers C.W.	— " —	B/186
	38044	Y/Bdr	White A.R.	— " —	— " —

Casualties for June 1918.

2/Lt		A. R. Davies	
56568	Sgt	Flynt A. J.	
42300	"	Odkins J. C.	
40206	"	Laskey H. S.	
38000	"	Williams W. A.	
233688	Cpl	Saggers C. W.	
38193	"	Collins J.	
54829	Bdr	Ward G.	
217389	"	Skinner E.	
875597	"	Kirby H. G.	
796916	L/Bdr	Mackam W. T.	
27646	"	Agres J.	
129774	"	Wenn W. H.	
21008	"	Asby C. A.	
168435	Fitr	Boast J.	
38267	Gnr.	Grace M.	
59489	"	Mundy R.	
145878	"	Nuttall C.	
242888	"	O'Neil H.	
230576	"	Hallwood J.	
208861	"	Yates J. S.	
42872	"	Bentley E.	
228109	"	McLuglan G.	
236123	"	Hubbutt J. P.	
243318	"	McNulty P.	
38067	"	Robson R. A.	
656689	"	Miller E. G.	
201368	"	Jones J. C.	
1638	"	Coomber J.	

All above B/186 Gassed on 2/6/18

105887 Gnr. Isherwood W. A/186. Gassed 2/6/18.

25744 Cpl. S/S May J. A/186. Wounded 4-6-18.

47654 Bdr. Balsdon C. } A/186
15547 Gnr. Packham J. } Gassed 5/6/18

38336 Bdr. Crawshay H.
38130 Gnr. Hopkins J. W. H. } C/186
204193 " Proud J.   } Gassed
204204 " Taylor W.   } 7-6-18.

187631 Gnr. Nuttall N. G. A/186. Gassed 16-6-18.

37783 Gnr. Duffield B. C/186 Wounded 16-6-18.

Wynne Lt. Col. R.F.A.
Comdg 186 Brigade R.F.A.

186 Brigade RFA

War Diary

July 1918